CW01080194

# 50 Ways to Master
# British Sign Language
# for Equality and Connection

# 50 Ways to Master British Sign Language for Equality and Connection

## Kirsty Walker

Thank you for
Your Support x

Enjoy Reading
♡

2021.

Published by Kirsty Walker

© Copyright Kirsty Walker

50 WAYS TO MASTER BRITISH SIGN LANGUAGE
FOR EQUALITY AND CONNECTION

ISBN 978-1-5272-8682-5

Typeset in Bembo by
Palimpsest Book Production Ltd, Falkirk, Stirlingshire

Printed and bound in Scotland by Bell and Bain Limited, Glasgow

# Contents

# Contents

# About the Author

Kirsty Walker was born in Scotland and left at a young age to live in Australia. Returning to the UK at the age of 19, she worked in the family's pubs, then as a nanny, before qualifying as a nurse. She is also a Reiki practitioner and has a diploma in Sound Healing Massage therapy. She has a three-legged dog, Lily Pily Rose, who jumps more now than she did with four legs and is insanely jealous of the cats, Zeus and Persephone.

Kirsty's BSL journey started from a life-changing accident. While recovering she decided to enrol on a free eight-week introduction to BSL course and instantly fell in love with the language. Despite a bumpy start to her journey while studying at University level, she let nothing get in her way. Her determination led her to seek an alternative route and today she is qualified to level 3 BSL.

This is Kirsty's first venture into publishing. She feels that she has a unique take on BSL and how to learn it. She has all of this information in her head and wants to share it to show you that you can do it too. Together we can break down the barriers to equality.

*If you ever want Botox you might want to consider learning a different language.*

**Kirsty Walker**

*It's a journey. No one is ahead of you or behind you. You are not more 'advanced' or less 'enlightened'. You are exactly where you need to be. It's not a contest. It's life. We are all teachers and we are all students.*

**Seema Mishra**

I dedicate this book to my son, Connor, whose honesty, courage and strength inspires me. His ability to always be true to himself is the reason this book exists.

I also dedicate this book to Bryan.
Wonderful Kind Funny Genuine Good man god you.
Thank you.
Bryan is one of life's gems.

# Introduction

I once described learning British Sign Language (BSL) as constantly taking part in *The Generation Game* where everything that goes with learning the language went past me on a conveyor belt as I frantically tried to grab at it and discover who I am as a signer. It's tough. But I want to show you it does not need to be this way through 50 easy tips to help you connect with signs, important information to remember and think about, help with handshapes, fingerspelling and much more. This is purely through experience and is simply designed to show you ways that helped me. Even if you take one tip and pass it on to another person, then the aim of the book has been achieved but more importantly you have moved one step closer to your goal and we have all moved one step closer to equality. There will be something in here that speaks to you. Throughout there will be technical terms used which are some features of BSL and are used within examples. This is not an academic book by any means and I have not elaborated, so please ask your teacher; or you may already be covering these aspects of the language or about to start. If you are not studying BSL yet, consult relevant literature. This book can assist as an extra study tool alongside being taught by the experts on your course or, if you are thinking about studying BSL, it will give you an understanding of what you are about to embark on and ignite that spark you have. You may already be communicating with someone where BSL is not completely necessary but on some level is used, maybe in your work with the elderly, and you can use some of these tips to help communicate with each other better.

# Before You Start

1. Sign language is at the heart of Deaf culture, their community, customs and values. This is the single most unifying characteristic. You do not necessarily need to be amazing and fluent, but what is vital is accepting BSL as a language in its own right and respecting this. Learn about big D and small d, Deaf culture, values and customs. Their directness, thumping on floors or tables, their physical proximity, pointing, eye contact, touch and so much more. Understand the ways in which they have been discriminated against, how the education system has failed them, and how society fails them both now and in the past. I urge you to take a look through the history of their community and follow it through to today to fully appreciate it.

2. Find a great teacher. Maybe enquire into a local course. I had an amazing teacher, Bryan Marshall, and it is down to him that I am where I am today.

3. Do not avoid the hard part of learning the grammar and from the outset grasp it. You can learn all the signs you want but where are you going to put them. This leads me on to Sign Supported English (SSE). Although

used in some situations, where you are signing with hearing people learning BSL, discourage SSE. You want to remain in BSL mode and not, when it becomes too difficult, default to SSE. Honour the beautiful language and culture BSL offers and stick with it.

4. Have a look at top tips for communicating clearly. You will find an abundance of information on the internet through resources and organisations. This will kick-start your confidence.

5. I know this may sound strange but even if you come across this once or a few times it will help. Know your geography and where the continents and countries are in relation to the globe. Trust me, it is so much easier to sign when you have a good understanding and can point to and describe the shape of a continent or country.

6. Lastly, if you haven't already, learn the alphabet.

# Useful Resources

BSL Dictionary (On-Line)
British-sign.co.uk
Bsl/zone.co.uk
Spreadthesign.com

**On Facebook** –
BSL Word Search Puzzle Book
Practice makes perfect (open)
Deaf BSL Chat
Sign BSL
SignConnect
My Sign

**On Instagram** –
Bsl zone
Signislandbsl (this is an amazing one – I love it and great for
    fingerspelling practice)

**On television** –
*See Hear* on BBC2 at 8am on the first Wednesday of every
    month

# How to Use This Book

The best way to use this book is to read it from the beginning to the end going from tip 1-50. It won't take long and you'll gain an understanding of how the tips can help you and which are the ones that best suit your needs. It will also help you identify any goals you wish to set. You'll find some lined pages at the back of the book for you to write down some goals. You could head straight to the list of tips at the back of the book and choose from there. The majority of the tips in the book will have tasks for you to complete on the pages provided. If you complete them they will be useful tools for reflecting on your own self-development and keeping track of any goals you've set. It will be important to take the book everywhere to record your learning. You will have light-bulb moments and start to see the world through the lens of BSL.

Hopefully this book will be an extra, self-study, tool for you during those long hours of study you have to put in. It will help you learn faster and show you how to think, feel and breathe BSL.

# Terminology Used

You will learn about linguistics when studying BSL in more depth than I shall go into here. I just want to offer some simple descriptions of the terminology used throughout the book. This will help you understand the tips more clearly.

**Roleshift** – when you shift into someone else and take on their identity or mannerisms for the sake of describing or to tell a story.

**Fingerspelling** – is simply where you spell out words on your fingers using hand movements.

**BSL word order – Phonology — Syntax — Semantics**
Phonology = sign pattern, handshape and placement, movement, direction, orientation, non-manual features.

Syntax = sign order – time frame – topic★ – comments – action(s) – question(s) – period (when)★.

★The placing of the time frame is flexible. You could state the time frame at the beginning or at the end but you must always set up the topic first.

Semantics = the meaning.

**Setting up the topic** – This is as it sounds. You set up the topic of the conversation you are about to have before going on. This is a feature of BSL word order (see above★).

It's the most important step in starting a conversation, so that the receiver knows what you're going to be talking about.

**Facial expression** – This comes under the umbrella of non-manual features, which include the eyes, mouth, torso, cheeks, head and shoulders. They are tools you can use to convey meaning in BSL.

**Mouth patterns** – are also grouped under non-manual features. You can mouth English words without using your voice to help clarify some signs. You also have mouth gestures where you can express meaning, emotions or actions.

**Handshapes** – are basically the shapes your hand/s will take to form words and describe objects, people and places. Your handshapes need to be accurate and clear as it can change the meaning of the signs. It's like pronouncing a word incorrectly.

**Describing** – is where you use a combination of handshapes, mouth gestures, and facial & body expressions to describe anything you need to.

**Signing space and placement** – is the space at the front and side of you. Imagine it as like standing inside a square picture frame with the back of the frame on your lower back with your elbows to the side of it. This is where you will place (known as placement) people, objects or buildings throughout your story. It's important that you refer back to where you placed the object by pointing or the gaze of an eye.

# TIPS 1 – 17

# Learning BSL

# TIP - 1

## One of the Best Ways to Learn

*Love yourself first because that's who you'll be spending the rest of your life with.*

*Anon*

This is difficult but so important and useful. I found it one of the best ways to learn.

Practise in front of the mirror and/or record yourself to watch back.

You will notice so much –

1. How your body moves.
2. Handshapes, are they loose?
3. Are your signs too close or too far apart?
4. Is there a nice flow between signs?
5. Are your facial expressions mirroring your roleshift, body movements and sign/s and, importantly,
6. Are you relaxed and putting all the aspects of the language together?

But remember no one will see you the way you see yourself so do not be critical of yourself.

Look at your qualities. We are all unique. So many times I've heard, 'they are a better signer' or 'they aren't good at role-shift or facial expressions.' It never made sense to me, it is a language not a competition! How can we all be the same? How boring would that be!

After watching yourself, write a list of your amazing qualities and the bits you feel you need to work on. Maybe you can work towards a goal on the goals page at the back of the book.

_____

_____

_____

_____

_____

_____

_____

_____

_____

_____

# TIP - 2

# How to Start Thinking in BSL

Look at a newspaper, magazine or the book you are reading and choose a sentence to change from English to BSL. Over time increase from one sentence to two, then more. Always start easy.

I made a promise to myself to change one sentence a day using BSL word order. I kept a notebook of all my sentences and referred back to them.

This also helped when I had to sign a story or was useful when practising with fellow signers as I could sign my sentences to them and it was always a great feeling, for both, when the receiver knew what I signed.

Below is the BSL word order —
**Timeline — Topic — Comment/Action —**
**Question — Period (when)**

Here is an example of how you could use it. Remember the placement of the timeline is flexible —
**yesterday — weather — awful**

Another example –

**car — broke down — garage phone — yesterday**

> **Record your sentences here that you have changed from English into BSL word order.**
>
> _____
>
> _____
>
> _____
>
> _____
>
> _____
>
> _____
>
> _____
>
> _____
>
> _____
>
> _____
>
> _____
>
> _____
>
> _____
>
> _____

# TIP - 3

## Another Way to Think in BSL and Learn BSL Word Order

Here is another way to help learn BSL word order. Draw a picture and set the scene up, for example –

A man climbing up a hill. You would not draw the man; it would need to be the hill first.

You would then not sign climbing as you would need to mention who is climbing –

1st (**insert basic outline of a hill**) Hill

2nd (**insert stick man figure**) Man

3rd (**insert stick man figure climbing the hill anywhere on the hill**) Climbing.

Remember, start talking to yourself in BSL, not English. Walk around the house describing a story or using your sentences and stories. You can be anywhere visualising a story or conversation in your head.

It can feel like a safer place at first in our heads. Use inside your head wisely. You have an opportunity to master it in there before putting it out in the open.

Draw some of your own pictures here and write underneath them in BSL word order.

# TIP - 4

# Facial Expression

*Take risks: if you win, you will be happy; if you lose, you will be wise.*

*Unknown*

Facial expression is such a vital part of sign language. It's like your face carrying out an action, expressing your attitude or that of someone else. It can be used to describe how the action was done. It can be difficult for us hearing people, when learning BSL, to fully understand how important it is. We've never had to rely on our faces to express such a huge depth of meaning in order to convey a message.

Our facial expressions need to link with our heart and gut. This is the driver for our emotions. If we harness this connection our experiences can be conveyed with our face.

It is important not to force facial expression to happen from the outset as it will naturally happen when all the aspects of the language start to come together and your confidence grows. We naturally have expression and then we throw an expression on top of it. Coupled with 'am I getting it right' the result can be a disaster.

My teacher wasn't very focused on my facial expression. He created a safe, non-judgemental space for it to develop naturally. He let me experiment with what felt right, at my own pace. I started learning BSL at university and for several weeks they would have us practising facial expressions. We had to stand up in front of the class and make facial expressions for others to figure out what they were. By the end of the experience I was beside myself. Firstly, because I wasn't connecting with any emotion. Nothing was there – just a funny face to pull. Secondly, I developed a negative mindset and this distracted me from the language. 'If I can't get my faces right, how am I ever going to do this, how will I ever convey meaning?'

Facial expressions are a form of non-manual features – non-verbal communication. They convey social information, be that emotions or an indication of intention. You've been doing this since birth. Think of it as tuning a piano – once tuned each note conveys its true meaning.

You might think you are getting it wrong but the majority of time you won't be. It's just difficult to use our faces in such a different way. Of course, we've always used our faces. Facial expression is a vital mode of communication in the speaking world too. Learning to *rely* on our faces so much more is the hard part. Eventually you won't even need to think about it.

# TIP - 5

## Combatting Fingerspelling

Okay. So, the dreaded fingerspelling.

The best tip I can give you is regular practice. It may also help to know many people struggle with this.

I found moving the, usually static, word from the realms of pages and screens to dynamic, animated hands the most difficult aspect of BSL.

Watch videos on fingerspelling and figure out what is being spelt or look at the answer first, then watch it over and over again.

The latter of these techniques helped me overcome my frustration. I would get so frustrated with fingerspelling and trying to figure out the word I would have to start over and over again countless times. I would talk to myself half way through, say the letters out in my head, look down at my hands for the I O U fingers while trying to put them on an invisible piece of paper with invisible letters on it. Eventually I gave up, finding an excuse not to practise fingerspelling until next time, which resulted in the same scenario.

I found knowing the word first relaxed me and I could focus on the mouth patterns and finger movements and eventually my brain started to recognise patterns.

Sometimes I even figured the word out by mouth pattern

alone or before the fingerspelling had finished again, as I started to link finger movements and mouth patterns together.

**Write down the words you learned how to fingerspell. Now practise these regularly. Choose a word a day or a week.**

_____

_____

_____

_____

_____

_____

_____

_____

_____

_____

_____

_____

_____

# TIP - 6

# Fingerspelling

To help with fingerspelling try spelling everything and anything you see whenever you have a spare moment.

Go slow. Speed will develop naturally over time. There is no need to force it!

Connect with your fingerspelling. Get a nice flow going between your fingers. Ask your teacher roughly how close together your hands should be. Get them to show you because it's far easier to be shown visually instead of having it described in a book.

Again, let your brain connect with the patterns.

You may look at your hands at first. That's natural. When you feel like you are ready, progress to looking away from your hands, then even close your eyes, and practise.

As always, start small and progress slowly.

Then try patterns. See how every word can be broken down into patterns of hand and finger movements. You can break down some words by the syllable. So one syllable becomes one pattern, you have a brief pause then move on to the next pattern.

Now try these four exercises. Trust me, they work!

**BOSTON (2 patterns) = BOS (quick pause) TON**
**BADMINTON (3 patterns) = BAD (quick pause)**
**MIN (quick pause) TON**

Try these two-letter combinations to develop a flow:

**Th — he — an — re**
**In — on — at — st**
**En — of — hi — as**
**To — ed — te — or**

Try these reversing words to help strengthen flow between letters. It helps your brain develop those patterns that will make your fingerspelling more fluent:

**WAR — RAW**
**WON — NOW**
**PAT — TAP**

On the go, when you see something spell it. If you are sitting on a bus, train or in the park, practise them and always add to your list.

_____

_____

_____

_____

_____

# TIP - 7

## Label Your Action

If you have role-shifted, label it. Tell yourself that is what you have done. Do the same with describing and facial expressions. This can be while you're signing or outwith your studies. You could practise on:

Mondays - noticing and recording when you or others have role-shifted.

Tuesdays - describing day, even verbally describing something to get yourself used to taking in extra details. Notice what feelings and emotions this stirs in you.

Wednesdays - notice and record when you or others used facial expressions to convey a message or express an emotion. Can you tell what emotions are being conveyed when you're sitting a distance away from them?

**Label your or others' actions and think about how you came to this conclusion.**

---

---

---

---

---

---

---

---

---

---

---

---

---

---

---

---

---

# TIP - 8

## Ways to Use Your Body

If we're feeling positive or expressing something that delights us our eyebrows will be raised, which naturally widens your eyes. Your body could come forward because if something is positive we tend to move or lean forward.

If we're feeling negative our eyebrows move down, natu- rally creating a frown and those lines between our eyes (don't botox those lines you need them). You might move your body back because if it is something we don't like we naturally pull away.

If you're confused you might move slightly sideways and tilt your head to the side.

You're probably thinking: this is so obvious! I do this without even thinking. When you're learning BSL, though, your aware-ness of these things is heightened. The subtlety of our body movements and expressions take on a whole new meaning. A Deaf person will be acutely in tune with these subtleties too. You could be signing away but have something on your mind that is troubling you. No doubt this will manifest in your body in some way and the receiver will pick up on it.

An opportunity to develop awareness and mindfulness presents itself. Think with your eyes. Take it all in and let it flow through your hands. After all, your hands are your mouth.

Feel the texture of what you see. Look for the patterns. Does it remind you of a childhood memory, with your gran maybe? Really take it all in. All the finer detail and how that makes you feel. Then express how it makes you feel and it will come out through your signs.

# TIP - 9

# Connecting With Your Feelings Through Your Stories

I think this tip is important because when we are given stories to translate from English to BSL and they are not our own personal accounts it can make it difficult to connect with what we are being asked to communicate.

It will be easier to express and connect with your feelings and emotions through your own stories. In turn this will naturally create a reflection of your true facial expressions and body movements without it being forced or worrying if the sign is consistent with your facial expression, roleshift and body movements.

When I experienced nerves and was trying to remember what was asked of me, looking down at the story interrupted the flow and cut eye contact with the receiver.

The more you practise with your own stories, the more natural and comfortable you will feel expressing yourself.

Write a story here that you connect with and
practise the same story over and over again to
build your confidence expressing yourself
through your hands, body and facial expressions.

_____

_____

_____

_____

_____

_____

_____

_____

_____

_____

_____

_____

_____

_____

_____

_____

# TIP - 10

## Observational Skills

Put your television on mute and watch your programme, for however long you want, observe mouth patterns, facial expressions and body movements.

Just relax and observe everything, the full scene. What time of the day is it, judging by what they are doing, leaving work or going to work? What season is it? How can you tell? Is it by what they are wearing? Are people arguing, is something happening? Is there a breeze? If so how would you know that?

Enjoy when you know what is happening.

What did you pick up from watching the programme in silence? Write down how you knew what was happening. This is important so you can connect and observe what you understand and have learned in other situations.

_____

_____

_____

_____

_____

_____

_____

_____

_____

_____

_____

_____

_____

_____

_____

_____

# TIP - 11

# More Observational Skills
# to Help With Roleshift

Watch comedians. They are great at roleshift which is such an important part of BSL. Although their roleshift sometimes can be over-exaggerated you will equally get a good idea of roleshift. Do not put your television on mute when watching comedians role-shifting as it will help to hear their voices slightly shift also.

Now try this – after watching with the sound on, watch the same sketch with no sound. Was anything different? Did you notice further detail? Think about what it was like watching it with two senses, then just one – your eyes.

**Write your answer below**

_____

_____

_____

_____

# TIP - 12

# Learning Through Facial Expression, Body Movement and Roleshift

Watch video clips online of people signing but don't try and understand what the conversation is through the signs. Instead, try and understand the conversation through –

1. Facial expression. The eyes, mouth and eyebrows.

2. Body movements. Are they leaning back or forward or to the side? Are the shoulders going up or down? Are they open or closed?

3. Mouth patterns. Do you recognise any common mouth shapes? The lips - did they move up at the edges or were they pouting? Are they pursed? If so, how tightly? This could indicate frustration or disapproval. Do the eyes match the pursed lips?

4. Was there any roleshift? Did you see slight changes in their body and if so did they appear to be different from moments ago? Maybe they have taken on a more masculine role, a more feminine role?

Now have a look at the comments, if there are any, and see if you were correct or on the right track and if there are comments look at the word order.

Watch anything you can and observe everything, learn from others, even actors and performers, watch movies or go to see Deaf-friendly plays.

---

**Write down what you picked up from the video clip, or anything else you have watched, through their facial expression, body language, mouth patterns or roleshift. Now record how. How did you know? What did their face tell you? Or maybe you noticed their body looked tense, then their shoulders and facial expression confirmed your observations.**

_____

_____

_____

_____

_____

_____

_____

_____

_____

# TIP - 13

# Repetition, Repetition, Repetition

*Repetition of the same thought or physical action develops into a habit which, repeated frequently enough, becomes an automatic reflex.*

Norman Vincent Peale

This might sound exhausting but it helped me so much as it left me on a positive note and feeling accomplished. It particularly helped when I had moments of wondering what on earth I was doing and felt overwhelmed by it all.

If I got a sign wrong or needed one confirmed when signing a sentence or story or simply having a conversation, I would start back at the beginning and re-sign it all.

This obviously was within reason and not when I was half way through a story. So, if you're well into a story, start back at the sentence or a few signs before you got it wrong. I found that doing this repetitive action not only helped me learn the sign in question but BSL word order, signing space and the other aspects of the language.

This tip helped me squeeze in that extra bit.

# TIP - 14

## Help With Handshapes

As you progress you will learn handshapes are important and can change a story completely if the handshape/s is/are wrong or too loose. Having loose handshapes is like mumbling a word.

To help with this, put a bottle in your hand and now take it away and hold the shape. Try with other objects, a mobile, fridge handle, handle on your chest of drawers or any other object you wish.

What does your handshape look like? Where are your fingers and thumb?

Put a pen in your hand, how do you hold it? It will be different for everyone.

Now try with tricky objects, ones that are tricky to replicate when describing. I believe in visualisation as an effective tool for learning.

Put the object in your hand, take it away and look at the shape you have created, close your eyes and continue to visualise it and create a detailed mental image of the desired outcome (your scene or object) and use all your five senses as well as your sixth sense, your internal feeling.

I use visualisation with exercise when I am not feeling motivated. I visualise myself doing the sets and adding weight.

I connect with how that makes me feel and set a goal. I visualise myself achieving the goal and the smile on my face at the end. This also allows me to connect with my feelings using the sixth sense to add extra visualisation.

In another tip I ask you to try an exercise with regard to describing and visualisation using your sixth sense to help with this.

**Write a list of tricky objects or ones you need to work on and practise when you can. You could also write down repeated handshapes you notice recurring in many other objects.**

_____

_____

_____

_____

_____

_____

_____

_____

_____

_____

# TIP - 15

# Self-Awareness Through Handshapes

As you know, self-awareness is having an understanding of your character and your feelings. When I mention it here, however, I mean self-awareness in a slightly different way. This different understanding will help greatly with your handshapes and their accuracy when having a conversation.

Imagine you're telling a story about a really heavy chair you had to move. You use only one hand when describing but you actually used two when you were heaving the chair across the room. Your fingers and hand are in a loose handshape when describing even though you had white knuckles from clinging to the chair so tightly. Your facial expression is relaxed and smiling even though you were red-faced, puffing and panting trying to drag this chair along. Do you see how this isn't painting an accurate picture of your experience?

Start to observe the way your hands move through the world. How do you turn the doorknob? All handles are different, what does your handshape look like? Are your fingers under the handle, sideways or over the top? Is there only room for three fingers or more?

What does your handshape look like when you hold an apple or a pen? Does your handshape change depending on how you feel? How, if at all, do you move your hands as an aid for expressing a feeling?

The more self-awareness you bring to the way you move through the world, the more depth and expression you can bring to BSL. This whole exercise is a wonderful mindfulness practice in itself. The more awareness we can bring to our present-moment experience, the less energy we feed those negative feelings or intrusive thoughts. It can be wonderfully grounding and settling to just move around your environment in a curious and present way.

## TIP - 16

## Handshape Experiments

Try these experiments.

Put your mobile in your hand. Pretend you are texting. Now take away the phone but keep the handshape. What do you notice? Where are your fingers and thumb? Now do the same with your TV remote control. Seem familiar?

How do you drive? Close your eyes and mentally visualise it. Now go and sit in your car as if you are driving. What do your handshapes look like on the steering wheel? Where are your hands placed on the wheel, where does your arm rest or are two hands on the wheel? Shoulders, is one relaxed more than the other, one slightly higher? How do you sit, slouched or up tall, slightly to one side? How close are your knees or yourself to the steering wheel or do you rest one arm on part of the door? Once you have it, write it down. In the hearing world, we are complacent. We don't fully connect with our senses, our minds fill in the gaps. Writing it down in as much detail as possible will really highlight the points you need to be thinking of. You're not just sitting in the car, really be aware of your full body and senses.

Write it down and compare it to your mental visualisation. Think about how you would describe this to the receiver.

Is it the same or close enough for the receiver to fully understand how you drive or hold a phone? If they were to repeat it back to you would it be accurate? Use visualisation and your five senses to achieve your desired goal; that is: what exactly do you want to get across to the receiver? Really embody your unique characteristics. The way you hold yourself, the way you move through the world. If you're talking about someone else you'll need to learn to become very observant. You'll notice also the unique ways in which all other people move through the world. This is the depth of detail you need to be aware of to make your BSL truly passionate and expressive.

Compare your findings from your visualisation to how you actually performed the task. Are there any differences? What are they and how would you do it differently next time?

_____

_____

_____

_____

_____

_____

_____

_____

# TIP - 17

# Mindfulness of Your
# Signing Space & Placement

The signing space is a nice tidy space from just above your head to just below your waist and out to each side just beyond your elbows. Think, if you were too high, too low, or too wide it would be like listening to someone darting all over the place – your head would be spinning just watching them!

Remember where you have placed objects, people or buildings in your signing space as it will look messy and chaotic to the receiver if you forget. Imagine it a bit like a messy picture scribbled all over the paper and you have no idea what it is.

For example, if you put the dog on the left then throughout the story always refer back to the dog on the left, unless he's legged it elsewhere and that is part of the story. If he hasn't moved and the story is ten minutes long, you must always refer back to the dog on the left otherwise your story and the information will be messy to the receiver. They'll be confused, will lose interest.

It would be like me telling you a story about my holiday in Barbados but every time I mention the location of the holiday I change it.

# Tips 18 - 24

# Describing

# TIP - 18

# Why Respect Describing?

When describing, make sure it is accurate. If you are describing sitting at a table then describe the *exact* (as much as you can) width and height, don't be sloppy with it. Don't take for granted that your receiver has an instant image in their head of exactly what you're talking about. This is not a place to cut corners. It's the difference between an engaging conversation and a frustrating one.

Remember, Deaf people have been master observers their whole lives, their language is visual. Describing something sloppily is like telling a half-hearted story with inaccurate information on the assumption they know what you mean. It will feel dismissive.

## Your eyes are your ears!

I think it is respectful to appreciate and take your time to learn the visual aspect of a Deaf person's communication. Learn to appreciate the amazing way information, sensations and emotions go through their eyes and flow out through their body and hands. Without that, communication would be very dull.

# TIP - 19

## How to Describe
## Something Far or Close

If you had to sign about a noise you heard and you had to describe it being far away or close, how would you do that? Spend a moment thinking about this now.

If it was far away, then you would move your hand and arm fully outstretched. You don't need to push it as far as it will go, wiggling it about in an effort to push it even further. Outstretched is an ample way to describe the noise being far away. Then you would bring your hand and arm towards your ear at whatever angle the noise came from. From the left or right, behind or in front of you.

If the sound was close, use your arm to indicate how close the starting point is within your signing space and again bring your arm and hand to the ear.

Think about how you would describe an object, building or shop that was far away, not too far, close or very close.

Now have a think about how to add facial expressions to complement this. Could your body be involved as well?

This is simply to help you think about ways you can convey meaning without relying on signs. It also highlights how

DESCRIBING

BSL can be very intuitive. Almost like, well yes, of course you would describe it that way!

At first try breaking it down –

1. Convey something being far away or close with your hand and arm.
2. Add facial expression into it.
3. Add body movements in.

Use this space to try to break down how to convey meaning. What are you trying to say?

_____

_____

_____

_____

_____

_____

_____

_____

_____

_____

# TIP - 20

## Help With Describing

Look at something, a bridge maybe. Is there water flowing underneath it, is the water choppy or calm? The stone-work on the bridge, are there any shadows reflecting anywhere? Trees, are they the same?

Now describe to a friend, your teacher or family member and see if they know what you are describing. You can make it simple – a house or car – but the main aim is to see if they know what you are describing. It will feel amazing if they do.

You could also get them to write down what you are describing. Have a look at the order they write it down in.

Is your story in order? Is it all over the place? Does it reflect what you were trying to get across?

Now I don't necessarily mean is it in BSL word order and don't get disheartened if they have no idea what you are describing but just try this and you will see what I mean.

You could also ask your children or niece, nephew or friends' children to describe something to you and see if you were right.

Maybe draw a picture, then describe it and get someone to draw a picture of what you are describing (remember the finer details).

Are they the same or close?

What did you describe? Ask your family or friends for tips on how you could have done it differently to make it clearer to the receiver. What did they find clear about your describing? Do they have any tips on how you could do it differently?

_____

_____

_____

_____

_____

_____

_____

_____

_____

_____

_____

_____

_____

_____

# TIP - 21

# Describing Objects

BSL pretty much took over my thoughts but switching my brain to think in sign language required thinking differently, and not just by grasping the word order but thinking differently about the things I looked at and saw on a daily basis.

Describe what you observe, visualise it mentally. I found closing my eyes helped, and let it flow through your hands.

Again, always start easy to help build confidence.

On the next page write down what you described and how, then weeks or months later, refer back and see if anything has changed, as in how you described it then to how you would now.

**What have you learned?**
**What would you change and why?**
**Do you look at things differently and how?**

Over time the reason I ask these questions will become clear.

What did you describe? Was it the angle that caught your eye or the bumpy textures? Remember to refer back at a later time to see if you would describe the same object differently.

_____

_____

_____

_____

_____

_____

_____

_____

_____

_____

_____

_____

_____

_____

_____

_____

## TIP - 22

## An Experiment Using Auditory and Visual Senses

Auditory stimulus reaches the cortex faster than the visual stimulus.

Maybe this is why hearing people are not as good at describing in finer detail. Imagine you were on the phone and you heard a car rushing past making an unbearable sound. You can tell it was driving fast without even looking. We may have made an assumption about who was driving it, what type of car and so forth. On your lunch break you tell your friend about the car. You add detail with the tone and inflection of your voice. You might have found the noise annoying or you've always had a pet hate for those souped-up boy racer cars.

But think if you had only *seen* the car. What detail would you add?

How would you express how fast it was going and how loud it was?

Did people look around, did they have annoyed or shocked looks on their faces? Because what facial expression is expressed will give a clear message about what others thought and this can add more detail for you to express. Even down to how fast they turned around or even how many people turned around, indicating so many people thought the same.

You thought other people were annoyed but why did you think that? Did the car have to brake hard at any point? Were other cars affected on the road? Was there smoke from the tyres? Was the road busy or not? Were lots of people around? The list could go on forever. Would you have verbally expressed any of these details if you just heard it or even if you heard and saw it?

So, slow your movements down (not in the sense of slow motion), really look at your handshapes, the object and scene. Try not to rely on your hearing as a true representation of the scene and/or situation. You're painting a scene with BSL for your receiver. Develop mindfulness of the infinite myriad of detail in any given situation. Try and talk with your eyes, tap into this sense instead of relying on hearing and seeing alone.

Use the next page to try your own experiments and watch something with both the auditory and visual sense, then just visual. Put headphones on. Write down your findings and compare the two.

I often wonder if what we see and touch is easier to remember than what we hear. If so, I wonder if that then connects us better to our gut feelings, which can then help us express ourselves more.

Maybe we just see objects for what they are. Like a cup, for example. We label it as a cup and it serves a purpose for us.

When we begin to visualise, though, you might have an expectation that you should 'see' things vividly. As an exercise, close your eyes and 'see' the room you're in with your mind's eye. Can you see the furniture and the colour of the walls? Do you still have a sense of how the room is arranged? That, in essence, is visualising. You might find that 'seeing' is more a kind of knowing what the space feels like with all of your senses. We are trying to move beyond the ordinary sense input of the hearing world. We are trying to open ourselves to new ways of expression and being.

**Try the car experiment I mentioned above and write your findings down. Remember you can come back to these at a later date and see if anything has changed or you would change.**

_____

_____

_____

_____

_____

_____

_____

_____

_____

_____

_____

_____

_____

_____

# TIP - 23

# How to Think in BSL
# Through Signs and Describing

With the signs you know put a story together while using the BSL word order. Create a lovely flow between the signs even if it is three, four or five signs. Now get creative and add in some more detail and start describing.

You could just use some of the sentences you've been putting together.

I would make up so many stories and be really creative with them, some were silly and over the top. I practised these at home while walking around the house or hoovering, ironing or cleaning, but the aim was to build my confidence and not rely on signs so much to communicate the meaning.

I did a story a week and continued to build on the same story or created new ones.

This tip will also help you start thinking in BSL with some added detail, for example, describing.

If you happen to be thinking about your story while ironing, follow the shape of the ironing board with your hands a few times to feel the shape. Now take your hands away and describe your ironing board. Don't forget to remove the hot iron!

Record your stories here. Did you use describing instead of a sign? Write down the objects you described.

_____

_____

_____

_____

_____

_____

_____

_____

_____

_____

_____

_____

_____

_____

_____

_____

_____

_____

# TIP - 24

# A Light-Bulb Describing Moment

As I've mentioned before, be sure to describe objects exactly as they are, not just flippantly describing with the assumption people will know what you are on about.

I had a light-bulb moment why the above is vital.

I was undergoing moving and handling training at work. We were being shown how to transfer patients on and off the hospital beds. Most of you will know that hospital beds are adjustable, they go up and down. If not, then the majority of us know roughly the ideal height of a bed because we want to be able to hop on and off without difficulty.

The trainer was talking about adjusting the beds and why it's important for nurses and patients. The beds only go to a certain height and as she was explaining important information about the height her hand was *way up* high (indicating the bed). Now I know, being a nurse, the safe height for the beds but I thought – well, if this was being interpreted for others and her hand is up that high the importance of safety for the nurses and patients does not match because that is a very dangerous bed to get in and out of!

This just illustrates the importance of being mindful and attentive with your describing. You can see here how you would be giving very conflicting information to the receiver. Just remind yourself of this when you're in conversation.

Write down where you have noticed the information spoken has not matched the action/description. This could be anywhere, watching TV, walking in a park or out having dinner.

_____

_____

_____

_____

_____

_____

_____

_____

_____

_____

_____

_____

# Tips 25 – 32

# About Signs

# TIP – 25

## Dealing With Multiple Signs

You will find out quickly that there are many signs for one word.

So my advice is to learn one (for your region) and connect with it. Do not get bogged down with all the rest as over time you will start to learn what the other signs are the more you come in contact with BSL users and progress further into your studies.

Although I said above learn one and connect with it, please do also be flexible. I just mean do not overwhelm yourself to begin with as you have so much to learn and think about.

In a BSL class a gentleman used some signs differently from what I have been taught. So I adapted to his way of signing. My point is that I was being flexible and using his way of signing as an exciting opportunity to grow my vocabulary.

You can always fingerspell if you are unsure what the other person is signing but importantly –

Ask your teacher for advice, ensure you have the sign correct with the correct handshape and be confident and stick with it.

**If you want to know all or some of the other signs for the one sign do your list here.**

_____

_____

_____

_____

_____

_____

_____

_____

_____

_____

_____

_____

_____

_____

_____

_____

_____

# TIP – 26

# Why Signs Are Tapped
# Once or Twice

Think about why some signs are either tapped once or twice or movements of signs are fast, slow, move two or three times forward and so forth.

We can tell a lot about what someone could be thinking or are thinking by their eyes, how quickly the body moves forward or backwards. Even from a young age what our parents' looks meant or how they turned around, sharply or gently, before 'getting that look', we knew how much trouble we were in. If in a foreign country we can tell if we have annoyed someone or if they are silently, inside, laughing at us because we tried to speak their language and got it badly wrong.

One technique to help me connect with the sign/s is to think of the above as tones in body language and through movement. The tone and movement is a bit like sound waves, where the vibrating air causes the human ear-drum to vibrate, then the brain interprets this as sound. I transferred that over to sign/s.

For example, have a look at the signs for director, manager, teacher, boss, why, because. How many taps or movements do they each have?

Now say the words (ones mentioned above) and tap and move the sign according to the correct way.

Say why and tap once, then say why and tap twice (as it should be). What feels better? By that I mean the sounding of the word that correlates with the sign (not if it is the correct way to sign it, with one or two taps).

What about because, two taps, be – cause.

What about information. Say the word, sign it appropriately and then say it again and sign it with just one or maybe two movements.

I hope this makes sense. If it does not it may at a later time, so keep referring back to this tip and you will eventually understand.

And please remember I do not under any circumstances mean the above is the theory behind why some signs are tapped once or twice or their movements. It is simply a way I thought of to help me grasp the sign and connect with it and hopefully it helps you too.

What sign/s are tapped once or twice? Think about why. Pronounce the word. Hear the tone in the word and reflect it through the sign.

_____

_____

_____

_____

_____

_____

_____

_____

_____

_____

_____

_____

_____

_____

_____

_____

# TIP - 27

## You Don't Always Need Signs

Unless you are in formal situations where predominantly signs are necessary, try not to rely on signs so much when having a conversation. This is important to understand. You'll be surprised how little signing you'll actually do sometimes.

When I was volunteering helping Deaf people learn English one of my students was telling me about his holiday. The story lasted roughly five minutes and throughout he only used something like four signs and this was only to set up the topic. Through facial expression, handshapes and body movements the story was easily conveyed. It was beautiful to watch and, of course, a lovely story about his holiday.

To make this point even clearer, I urge you to go online and search for BSL poetry. You'll enjoy watching them, I'm sure. See if you can pick up the signs used. Write down the ones you know or how many they used. Especially watch how they don't use signs to convey their message. What else did you pick up from the poetry? Think about the ways a message was conveyed without signs.

What have you conveyed today without using signs? Observe other people around you, on the train, in the coffee shop, and see if you can understand messages they are conveying. Or use this space for the exercise I asked you to do while watching BSL poetry.

_____

_____

_____

_____

_____

_____

_____

_____

_____

_____

_____

_____

_____

_____

_____

_____

# TIP - 28

# Think Before You Sign

Think before you sign. Do you really need to?

Have a think about this scenario; you are sitting across from your friend in a library and you are not allowed to talk. They have a nice cup and you want to let them know you like it. Instead of signing you could just point to the cup, raise your eyebrows and smile, or nod, and slightly lean your body forward.

Have you ever been in a clothes shop and your friend holds up a piece of clothing, you are across the other side of the room and don't want to shout your opinion about it for everyone to hear?

How do you convey your message? How could they let you know it's expensive or such a good price? What if it's expensive and you think, no way are you buying that! How would you get that across?

We have all been communicating like this since we were toddlers without even knowing what we were doing is such a vital aspect of BSL. You've had plenty of years of practice without even knowing. We have also been roleshifting for countless years without even knowing. Imagine you are sitting on your lunch break and your boss has been giving you a hard time. You are chatting away, venting to your friend about your boss. Your tone and inflection changes, you mimic your boss's voice. You have now role shifted into your annoying boss.

Here is another example of where we do not need to heavily rely on signs.

We were doing an exercise in my BSL group. Someone had signed that when they are driving on a long journey on straight roads they sit a certain way in their car for comfort. Which was great, I was very proud but it was a very formal way of signing so I suggested using fewer signs. Firstly by setting up the topic, which took one sign. Then I moved my body into a comfy position, while my face conveyed the message it was a long journey and a bit boring. This way of using BSL is much more natural and expressive than just signing.

**Think of other ways you might have been doing this before you knew about roleshift. Have you seen or heard other people roleshifting?**

_____

_____

_____

_____

_____

_____

_____

_____

_____

_____

_____

_____

_____

_____

_____

_____

_____

_____

# TIP - 29

## Think About Where
## to Place the Sign

Try not to focus on getting the sign/s right the first time or even all the time when learning BSL. You are going to be on a long journey, learning new signs for the rest of your life and career.

Just take your time and think about what a new sign might be – visualise it. Think about where the sign would be placed around the body. If you had to work out the sign how would you describe it first? Over time your confidence will grow and you'll develop the ability to figure out a sign (rightly or not) without looking it up first.

I'll give you a good example. I was explaining to my teacher, one day, that I practise Reiki. There is no sign for this (well, not that I've managed to find) so I finger-spelled it, setting up the topic. I put my hand in the appropriate shape in relation to the shapes we commonly see when looking at chakras in books. I moved from the first chakra down to the seventh, adding further details such as its colour, as I worked my way down.

So, you can see this was a bit improvised but the point made it across to my receiver. You can definitely get a bit creative with your BSL. Any language, and especially BSL, is a living organism. It likes to be stretched and adapted to new situations. Enjoy this process! It can be one of the most rewarding aspects of learning BSL.

**What signs did you learn by other methods other than looking for the sign/s online or asking?**

_____

_____

_____

_____

_____

_____

_____

_____

_____

_____

_____

_____

_____

_____

_____

# TIP - 30

## Thinking Again About Where to Place the Sign

From a previous tip where I asked you to think where the sign would be in relation to the body, here is another example of what I mean.

Legs and arms. I suppose they're obvious, right?

What about to dream, think, understand, not understand, or forget? Have a think about where you would place those signs.

All of these are signed around the head/brain area. So are some of the signs for mental health issues.

Husband and family are signed around the heart. If you were talking about someone else's husband you probably wouldn't sign it so close to your heart.

Love, jealousy and hatred are all about your emotions and are signed around the abdomen, chest, and heart.

Slow down and think about where the sign would be placed. Some are not so obvious and will leave you scratching your head. Another opportunity for mindfulness and embodiment presents itself here. Try to bring your attention the next time you feel a strong emotion like love or hatred to where the feeling presents itself in the body. If your sworn enemy walks past you with your ex happily holding their hand, do you feel that as a tightness in your chest or a sickness in your stomach? Don't be scared to explore your body and understand how your emotions affect your physical being. Not only will this improve the naturalness of your BSL but it will also help you to understand yourself more.

Here's a little challenge for you: what about the sign for spectrum? First think about what it means. Then think about how you would describe something in terms of its position on a scale between two points.

Now look up the sign for spectrum and see if you got it right.

Write the tricky ones down on the page provided for your reference.

**Which signs are placed where on your body? Remember to do the tricky ones.**

_____

_____

_____

_____

_____

_____

_____

_____

# TIP - 31

## Another Way to Connect With Signs

I would always get the sign for a person walking the wrong way around. Hopefully this helps you too.

So, when you were younger did you play puppets with your fingers? I would always draw the face on the soft pad of my finger. So just think of it like:

**Soft part = face**
**Hard part, the nail = back of the head.**

I now, unless I am describing walking backwards, know which way to place someone when walking along.

**Write ways you think about sign/s to help you retain them.**

_____

_____

_____

_____

_____

_____

_____

_____

_____

_____

_____

_____

_____

_____

_____

_____

_____

_____

# TIP - 32

## Connecting With the Sign

If you struggle with a sign, try to find a way to connect with it. A good example is the sign for remember. It's signed at the side of your head with a closed fist, like you're grabbing the information and putting it inside your brain.

Again it is like, I've got it, I understand it now, put it inside my brain.

Have a look at the sign for uncle. To me it makes no sense but try to understand it your way even if it's silly. It doesn't matter how you remember any particular sign because you will naturally come across some that are easier to connect with. Then for some reason for the life of you there will be ones you will always forget and can't remember and they will leave you scratching your head. It's all part of the journey.

Write down how you have remembered the sign that you find difficult to connect with. Use this as a reference to refer back to if you forget.

_____

_____

_____

_____

_____

_____

_____

_____

_____

_____

_____

_____

_____

_____

_____

_____

# Tips 33 – 40

# Handy Facts
# to Think About

# TIP - 33

# Reading the Theory for BSL

Understanding the theory is extremely important with anything we learn so we can put theory into practice. BSL is no different. However, try not and get so wrapped up in what the book says. Just relax. Read and understand it or just some bits or not anything at all but it's okay! You might not understand it all just now but give it some time. I made it harder for myself trying to remember and apply the theory side all the time. I missed the real part, the natural part – being able to communicate. So, read the theory, go and sign, watch videos, learn the language and every so often, at your discretion, go back and read the theory. It wasn't until months later I revisited the theory. I was surprised, not just at how far I had come, but how much more naturally I was understanding the theory.

Of course, we all know there needs to be a level of theoretical understanding but I found amongst the endless paragraphs of writing and explaining I was doing it all anyway, naturally. In fact, we have been all our lives. I am talking about our natural ability to communicate with others no matter the circumstances. There has always been more than just the spoken word.

This tip shows you that theory isn't everything, especially when you're just starting out. You'll soon be able to put the practice into what you are reading instead of the other way around.

# TIP - 34

## A Bit of Grammar

As you know, grammar is the whole system and structure of a language. So let's think about how grammar can be used in BSL.

In BSL, grammar can be expressed through our facial expression and handshapes for example:

**Big Ben**

**Getting biggER i.e. weight gain.**
**Growing biggER i.e. a child growing taller.**
**ER being the comparative.**

What I mean by this is —

**Big Ben - puffed out cheeks (facial expression) (x 1) plus your handshape will indicate big and it will be fixed as Big Ben is a fixed size.**

**Getting biggER - puffed out cheeks (facial expression) (x 2) plus handshape moving out and near the body area or all over where there**

**is weight gain, which will indicate the grammar 'ER' as in getting biggER.**

So think how can you express grammar to convey the meaning and/or what you are describing. Use the exercise box below to experiment.

Again this book is not academic and the above is another way to connect with the sign and understand why our facial and body movements and handshapes are so important.

---

**Write down signs where you can practise grammar.**

_____

_____

_____

_____

_____

_____

_____

_____

_____

_____

# TIP – 35

# Some Handy Things to Think About

**THINK**

Your dominant hand = the pen.

Your non-dominant hand = the paper.

Use your dominant hand to sign off from the non-dominant hand.

**THINK**

No flow from sign to sign is like speaking with no. Flow! And

Speaking? S l ow ly with

Dis jo int Ed words    it would    be really

Annoying!!!

**THINK ABOUT THIS**

If you want to convey to someone you were watching TV at home or a movie at the cinema you simply need to slightly tilt your head back. It's amazing how a slight tilt of the head can convey so much meaning. I'll show you:

Sit on your couch and look at the TV, remain sitting there and become aware of your full body. You will notice how you are sitting, your shoulders, where your legs are and the position of your head. Get a chair and sit in it like you would at the cinema. Become aware of your full body again from head to toe. Where now would you position your head? Think about why.

Because your TV screen is smaller and closer and placed at an appropriate level, your head is probably quite relaxed. But at the cinema your head would be anywhere from slightly to highly tilted back due to the size of the screen.

That simple tilt of the head is the equivalent of a spoken word. It's the distinction between telling your friend you watched a movie on TV last night or you went to the cinema. Micro detail is fundamental and serves as a foundation to effectively deliver any message.

What are the important finer details in some situations that have the power to change the meaning?

_____

_____

_____

_____

_____

_____

_____

_____

_____

_____

_____

_____

_____

_____

_____

_____

# TIP – 36

# 15 More Things I Think You Should Know

1. Signs = words
   Non-manual features = tone

2. Don't chew gum. It's annoying anyway – lip-smacking gum chewers. Moving your lips about in a random motion makes it very confusing to the receiver, especially if you are sitting there and the only thing moving are your lips.

3. Don't just sit there watching the signer, get involved and be an active listener.

4. Be honest! If you don't understand something, let them know. They will know that you haven't understood anyway from your body language – like a pro P.I.

5. BSL is not miming.

6. BSL is not just signs, you are not fluent because you know lots and lots of signs.

7. Don't waffle – stick to your point.

8. I like this one – when you pick your hands up to sign, say to yourself 'it's now time to think in BSL.'

9. Your brain will get tired – be good to yourself. Don't go too hard on yourself.

10. Don't just watch the signers sign, you will see them. Their body will speak louder than words.

11. Understand and connect with the sentence structure – know it well, then you can adjust it later.

12. Fingerspelling should only be used if there is no sign for the word (for instance, many names for places or people), if you need a sign clarified or, for the life of you, you have no idea what the sign is.

13. Learn some signs that will give you the confidence to approach BSL users and start a conversation such as – How are you? Name what? Live where? BSL level 1 learning. Dog have? Children have? Learn anything really that can be a conversation starter. You can end it there with a laugh and indicate, that's it! It will boost your confidence, trust me.

14. Go somewhere new. I say this as I had a lesson in a museum in Edinburgh. It was great to learn in a different environment, to give your mind and eyes new surroundings. I described the most beautiful staircase and at the end was a stunning window. I learned signs

for things that I normally would not have thought about learning while studying. We stood and each described a figure, whether in a painting or a display, and had to then look around and from the detail within the description point out the person.

15. Try to connect what you are doing while in BSL mode to what you do when you're in English mode. Write a list of all the things you have been doing your entire life to communicate that you are now being asked to do for BSL. I'm sure you will come up with many. For example, pointing is a  big part of BSL. How many times when giving directions or locating someone have you instinctively pointed? Or all the times you have had to describe in detail something for someone?

## TIP - 37

## Why Meet Other Signers?

You may get too familiar with the people you sign with in your group. When you meet other people they may sign differently, they may have a different dialect, or they may put heavy emphasis on English or mouthed words. Some might be difficult to understand while others might sign very quickly and it can feel like you are starting again from scratch. Although this is an important learning experience, it can knock your confidence a bit. It certainly knocked mine.

This tip is so important because if we close our minds to new approaches and differing opinions we don't learn. Simple as that. You will realise how much you do know and how much you can learn from others. Open your eyes to all the other ways you can communicate even if you don't know the signs!

If all else fails, at the very least, meeting other signers is a great way to get some fingerspelling practice in because you will have to ask 'sign what?' Or fingerspell the word to them. Don't forget your describing though!

What new sign/s did you learn from meeting new people? Did you learn anything else from them other than signs?

_____

_____

_____

_____

_____

_____

_____

_____

_____

_____

_____

_____

_____

_____

_____

_____

# TIP - 38

# Be Mindful of Changing Signs

Always keep yourself updated and adaptable. Over 550 new entries have been added to the *Oxford English Dictionary* in the first six months of 2020 alone. You can see how these things are constantly changing and moving. BSL is like any other language: it is constantly evolving and morphing. A language is an organic, living entity that is transmitted from person to person. Think of those friends we had when we were kids. We'd create our own languages, using words in a way that only we could understand.

With technology advancing and the world evolving, signs will change but also be mindful and respectful of some of the older signs. You might find some older adults will use traditional signs whereas the younger generation might be less likely to use traditional signs and have created many themselves.

You will also need to adjust your describing and facial expression and body movements in relation to the new change. For example, some trains are now electric therefore not as noisy and they feel more streamlined with less harsh jolting movement so you would not describe the train as being as noisy or as bumpy. Books too, with e-readers being very popular these days, can't be mindlessly described. We may take it for granted that for us a change of vocabulary is all that's needed to express that a person was reading an e-reader and not a book. It should be clear to you now that little things like this make all the difference in BSL.

Write down a list of old and new signs. What has changed and think about why? You could have fun with this and add it into your raising awareness night (as you'll go on to read about – have fun).

_____

_____

_____

_____

_____

_____

_____

_____

_____

_____

_____

# TIP - 39

## Useful Things to Remember When Learning BSL

Don't over-exaggerate your facial expression.

Don't over-exaggerate roleshift; it just needs to be a slight movement of the head, shoulders, waist or gaze.

You don't need to fully act out the character, person or animal you have roleshifted into. For example, putting in a contact lens. You don't need to fully pull your eyelid down showing all the white of the eye and grossing people out. Just place your finger under your eye as you have already set the topic up – this being contact lens. You'll find the balance between directness and subtlety in time.

If you are shifting into a dog, set the topic up with the sign. Shift your shoulders slightly in the direction the dog bolted off and ran. Now describe by facial expression and roleshift how the dog took off fast, jumped over the wall, and legged it.

Keep your signing and roleshift nice and neatly in your signing space. Try signing in your space then outside it and observe –

**What ones did you see?**

**How difficult were they? Even if you did see some outside your signing space were they easy to interpret?**

It's just as important for your handshapes to be correct while signing as when describing.

When you are signing and in a conversation if you look away for any length of time you will miss parts of the conversation. It is the same if we hearing people put our hands over our ears mid flow when in a conversation with someone.

**Write a list of things that are important to you to remember.**

_____

_____

_____

_____

_____

_____

_____

_____

_____

# TIP - 40

## Personal Space

Have you ever encountered people who get far too close and you have to take a step back? If they keep coming back into that space think how that makes you feel. Always think about your distance to other people when signing. Respect the signing space because the signing space is akin to personal space.

It will also make it difficult for both signer and receiver to see the signs, mouth pattern, body movements, facial expressions and roleshifts. You also run the risk of being smacked in the face!

The top tips for communicating will also be compromised if you are sitting in someone's personal space.

# Tips 41 – 50

# On a Personal Note

## TIP - 41

## Raising Awareness

Now, make sure you know what you're doing with your alphabet before starting this one. There is potential for much hilarity here. But we don't want to be going around telling people false information.

Show your partner, children, friends or even strangers the alphabet. Start with some basic signs or show them how to spell their name. This is an amazing way to help keep you refreshed with your signs while also raising your confidence significantly. It engages the other person too; you'll find most people are fascinated by BSL. Most importantly of all, of course, it raises awareness of BSL and the Deaf community.

You could also give them a history lesson on Deaf culture with information given to you by your teacher or relevant accurate material found online.

Why not have a myth-busting evening. Tell everyone facts about BSL. For example, most people won't know BSL has regional dialects. English is not a Deaf person's first language; in fact, it probably isn't even their second language. BSL is the preferred language for over 87,000 people in the UK while around 150,000 can use BSL. It has been recognised as Britain's fourth indigenous language. There is so much more you could talk about. BSL is a language with a beautiful, tragic and fascinating culture.

Always double-check your information is accurate! Have fun reading about Deaf culture and history.

A snowball effect can be started. If each of you raise awareness on a small level we can eventually raise the voice of the Deaf community to a larger audience.

I'll give you a few examples which just naturally happened to me. I was out for lunch one day, having a good catch-up, signing away. When I went to pay the bill the waitress mentioned she would love to learn BSL. She was mesmerised by the beautiful way BSL comes across. We exchanged emails and I sent her some tips on how to get started. Much like these ones.

Another time a barista approached me and told me he was learning BSL online. He told me how he was thrilled to see someone actually using it. On his break we sat down and spoke about BSL for ages.

I believe you should never just show someone how to do something, you should show them how to do it properly. I've been learning BSL for three years and every time I mention it there is always someone who says they would love to learn. That's a lot of people over the years! So where are we going wrong? There's a question for the government to answer.

Don't forget, add Tip 38 into your Raising Awareness night.

ON A PERSONAL NOTE

Write down the correct information you are going to pass on to your friends or family. Keep a note of what you have taught them.

_____

_____

_____

_____

_____

_____

_____

_____

_____

_____

_____

_____

_____

_____

_____

# TIP - 42

# Another Way to Raise Awareness

*A connection is the energy that exists between two people when they feel seen, heard, and valued; when they can give and receive without judgement; and when they derive sustenance and strength from the relationship.*

*Brené Brown*

I left Deaf history books out for friends and family, left BSL dictionaries strewn about, printed off articles about Deaf culture. I directed people to resources online or helped them sign their name.

I signed to my nephew, who was amazing, and he found it so much fun. I was always in awe at how easy it was for him to retain the signs. We would say a word and guess how it might be signed. I loved watching his facial expression and body language.

There are so many ways to raise awareness and get people involved. Anything just to ignite that spark in someone.

I especially love this story and it is a great example of the snowball effect. Just taking those small steps can make such a difference to someone else's life.

One week at a BSL class I taught every Thursday a new member of the centre's staff joined us. She hadn't long started working in the building and didn't really know anyone. She was especially keen to get to know the service users, though. One of the Deaf service users, Michael, who attended my class was a bit stand-offish, especially with new people. Before the class the new staff member had struggled to foster a connection with Michael. Just her turning up, having a real desire to learn and showing an interest in their history and culture made all the difference. Suddenly Michael would start approaching the new staff member to have conversations with her. He saw her as someone he could trust. She later approached me and was so grateful. She had no idea that doing such a small thing could make such a difference.

Write a list of ways you can raise awareness and how you want to. Then go and narrow the gap between the Deaf and hearing worlds. Remember always seek advice from the experts before doing so.

_____

_____

_____

_____

_____

_____

_____

_____

_____

_____

_____

_____

_____

_____

_____

# TIP - 43

## Your Personality?

Are you a tidy person, organised, and on time? Or the complete opposite; messy and unorganised? Observe your signs. Look in the mirror or at recordings of yourself and look at your signs. Do they reflect your personality? Are they too slow? Too fast? Too loose or with big wide movements? Are you outside the signing space?

**THINK**
**Should I adjust?**
**Should I tone down a bit?**
**Are my signs clear?**

The above is just about how you are getting your signs across. In spoken language if we're angry this can be heard in our tone. We don't necessarily need to see the other person's body language or face to know. It's the same for what we love and hate or what we agree with and don't agree with. They can be heard through tone and inflection. These are all influenced by our personalities, our values and what we want to share with the world.

So sometimes how the signs are conveyed can be driven by

our personality traits, which flow through the signs as a way of expression. As I said, our personalities can be intertwined so a good level of self-awareness may help.

I remember having lunch in a very busy café signing with a Deaf person. After we had finished eating, the waitress made it very clear she wanted us to leave so the next customers could come in. I described it with one hand as being shooed out. He described it with two hands and a step forward, as if being pushed out the café. Same situation, same story but two different personalities coming through. I am more laid back and had no issue with being shooed out, my friend wasn't as happy.

> **Think about how your personality comes through your signing. Write these down as it might help adjust or understand yourself more.**
>
> _____
>
> _____
>
> _____
>
> _____
>
> _____
>
> _____
>
> _____
>
> _____

# TIP - 44

# Go for it When Signing

*Sometimes we have to stop being scared and just go for it. Either it will work or it won't. That is life. Life is about jumping into the unknown and figuring out how to navigate through it. You can't wait for everything to be perfect or else you will be waiting forever.*

*Jayant Bhaga*

It is so important to trust yourself. Go with your gut instinct.

If you think that *might* be the sign, then go for it! Nothing is ever wrong, it's only ever an opportunity to learn.

I have learned so much by being wrong. The things I have learned through mistakes are ingrained in my mind now.

Please just trust yourself and laugh about it! Be proud that you made the effort! You'll get a lot of confused faces and a lot of laughs.

Trust me, I know! I got the sign for nurse and shit mixed up all the time. I was taught in Edinburgh. The difference between nurse and shit is so subtle I would often crack my teacher up.

**REMEMBER** don't let not knowing a sign hold you back.

I believe we miss so many opportunities by not taking a risk and putting ourselves out there. Good on you for trying to better yourself. Celebrate the triumphs then laugh and learn from the disasters. At least you're always progressing.

Oops! - What signs did you get incorrect? How can you remember and connect with it to get it correct next time?

_____

_____

_____

_____

_____

_____

_____

_____

_____

_____

_____

_____

# TIP - 45

# Confidence Boost

*Go easy on yourself. Whatever you do today, let it be enough.*
*Unknown*

Writing down the signs I was learning along the way in a notepad helped me hugely. I could always look at it on those days when I felt like learning BSL was an impossible task, like I knew nothing. I could see how far I had come. It gave me that boost I needed to keep going when I saw what I had achieved laid out on paper. It gave me an opportunity to go over the signs again, keeping them fresh in my mind. I could use it as a way to create stories or even just sentences to put in BSL word order.

It was a joy to see how much I had learned. Of course, there were some that I had totally forgotten. I tried to not think negatively or beat myself up. It's yet another opportunity to learn and grow. Remember to focus on how far you've come, how much you've achieved!

Even if you look at one sign a week, know it inside out, get it ingrained in your mind, and you'll feel amazing as you start to become a more confident signer.

Write the sign you want to learn this week before you move on to another. Remember to grasp it and connect with it before moving on to another one.

_____

_____

_____

_____

_____

_____

_____

_____

_____

_____

_____

_____

_____

_____

_____

_____

# TIP - 46

## Stepping Outside Your Comfort Zone

When we learn BSL it can be either in the comfort of our own home or behind closed doors in a room. Then we have to go out into the real world where many eyes will be on us. Believe me, people will stare A LOT.

So go to a coffee shop or wherever you feel you want to go as the main aim is to build your confidence while lots of people are around. Not only will this increase your signing confidence but you'll find it spilling into other areas of your life. It will increase your entire sense of confidence and ease in yourself.

This will help take you out of your comfort zone. You can start in a quiet place, then go busy.

Meet fellow signers or even friends or family who do not sign and sign away to them or help them learn a few signs but make sure you buy the coffee and cake as a thank you for helping you.

Then wherever you are –

**Sign**
**Sign**
**Sign.**

Record below places you could go to help step out of your comfort zone and build your confidence. You could have this as one of your goals.

_____

_____

_____

_____

_____

_____

_____

_____

_____

_____

_____

_____

_____

_____

_____

_____

# TIP - 47

## Taking a Further Step
## Outside Your Comfort Zone

Following on from Tip 46 to sign somewhere busy outside of
your home or the comfort of four walls. You could try stepping
outside your comfort zone and learn new ways to express
yourself by learning something new like –

Pole fitness.
Dancing. You could try Zumba or Salsa dancing, which is
   a wonderful way to express yourself.
Singing or whatever will push you and push you to express
   yourself more than you normally do or would have.

This will help with other aspects of BSL and your facial
expression and body movements.

Sorry, British people, but we (not all, of course!) can be re-
served, according to Google.

I remember I had to do a presentation in BSL, 6-8 minutes,
in front of two people while being recorded. I was so nervous.
To overcome this I sat in a coffee shop before the presentation
exam and recorded myself. I sat my phone up against my coffee

mug and signed away. Here I had a bigger audience than the two I was about to present to.

I found this very useful because you will quickly discover you have to express yourself and communicate differently through your body, hands and face; otherwise we may not get the meaning across.

**What have you always wanted to do but were too afraid? Can it help you with expressing yourself more?**

_____

_____

_____

_____

_____

_____

_____

_____

_____

_____

_____

_____

# TIP - 48

## Get Over it

*If you cannot do great things, do small things in a great way.*
*Napoleon Hill*

I remember having a lesson in a coffee shop and I could see a man watching us. I didn't feel annoyed as I didn't get the sense he was being rude. He was sitting relaxed, in a chair, coffee in one hand and his other hand resting under his chin, elbow on the table, with a gentle smile on his face. He was mesmerised and appeared to be enjoying the beauty of BSL as I caught his eyes watching the flow of signs. As it continued I started to realise that it was me with the hang-ups. It was only me that was worrying about what I looked like, was I good enough, was I doing it properly. This actually helped me get over myself! I thought 'well, it doesn't matter as I am doing my best and that will have the most profound impact.'

# TIP - 49

## Just Be You

*It takes nothing to join the crowd. It takes everything to stand alone.*
*Hans F. Hansen*

It is important to connect with who you are as a person when learning BSL. Inevitably, we'll get caught up in thinking others are better than us. Slow down and take a step back. Be true to yourself. Not the way you believe you should be. Be what feels right and intuitive. Honour what you are.

You don't need to add someone else's expectations of you to yourself. Losing who you are only adds an extra job to your long list.

You will start to build true friendships as the receiver will get a sense that you are at ease with yourself. The other person will get a sense of who you truly are, what your sense of humour is like, the little nuances that make you you. Someone who doesn't judge themselves won't judge you. Someone who accepts themselves will accept you. Someone who loves themselves will love you.

See how BSL is uniquely expressed through you. Then, hopefully, you'll learn more about yourself and see BSL as a way to love who you are.

Who are you? Write a list and stick to it. Go back and look at it if you are having a moment of feeling deflated.

_____

_____

_____

_____

_____

_____

_____

_____

_____

_____

_____

_____

_____

_____

_____

_____

_____

## TIP - 50

## What Now?

Through practising and applying the tips outlined in this book consistently throughout your studies and incorporating BSL into your daily routine, you'll achieve a steady growth in your knowledge and confidence. As you know, learning is a lifelong journey – so keep on keeping on.

The single most important aspect of BSL you will have cultivated to carry forward into the future is your hands. They will narrow the gap between the hearing and Deaf world. By doing so they can create new opportunities for themselves.

I now wish you all the best and I hope something in here has spoken to you. Through your journey you will discover you are not just learning a language, you are learning about a culture. You will be asking your body to move in so many different ways. So, embrace the beautiful combination of the many features working elegantly together in an utterly unique way, expressing who you truly are. So I am going to end here with telling you just one more thing: meditate. Keep going and don't ever think you can't do this because you can. Meditate until you remove yourself from your ego so you're still inside not adding any unnecessary negative thoughts to feed your ego. Keep going until you are nothing but a heartbeat.

From that very moment you will realise you can achieve anything because you are not your ego. You are a blank page where you can rewrite whatever and whoever you want to be. You don't have to be what others want you to be. Just:

**Meditate**
**And**
**Keep**
**Signing**

I have started learning Spanish, of course using some of my own tips for practising, and when I am struggling to remember a word (in Spanish) I start using BSL describing to help me connect with it. I also use my body to move with the pronunciation as Spanish is a very expressive language.

I love this story: When I was in Spain I was looking for a shop to buy a European travel adapter. I found a shop, it was big and had so much stock. I was tired and it was 37 degrees. The Chinese lady could not speak English and spoke to me in her native language. I really needed the adapter so I used the sign for the phone and pointed to the socket on the wall, described plugging the adapter into the socket and then another on top. I further described a thin cable going from one end and then into my phone which would light up my phone to use. She pointed me in the right direction.

I find it amazing that I am in Spain using BSL to convey to a Chinese lady what I need. Languages are so interesting and it goes back to what I said earlier, there has always been more than one way to communicate than the spoken word. We just need to open our minds to this and BSL can help you.

*Something I discovered on my BSL journey
when I stopped comparing myself to others,
when I walked away, was –*

*The best thing I did was stand alone.*

**Kirsty Walker**

# Goals

# Index of Tips

ON A PERSONAL NOTE